James Stordahl

The
KMA
Syndrome

A Grandpa Jim Blog

James Stordahl

The KMA Syndrome

James Stordahl

The KMA Syndrome

James Stordahl

CONTENTS

Acknowledgments

James Stordahl

ACKNOWLEDGMENT

My Bipolar-2 brain does not allow me to focus for long. It appears that years of therapy and medication is helping.

I have spent much of my life hiding. I have actively isolated myself from others. Only alcohol could help open the door to my brainpan. My own worst enemy took years developing.

I live with low self-esteem, anxiety, depression and bipolar disorder. I did not learn about the depth of this cluster of mental illnesses until my youngest daughter showed bipolar disorder tendencies at age 14. Her trauma and therapy got me very involved, and educated about mental illness.

Since jumping the mental illness "stigma" hurdle, I have questioned my education and my value-programming. Am I off base? Did I perceive training in an alternate universe? Never have I been so confused by the news. Never have I been more afraid for our democracy.

Nine grandchildren have also helped ground me. The 42 years of patient guidance and companionship of my wife, Charlotte, is also a major factor.

This book is my explanation of the turmoil I find myself in.

*My racing thoughts
continue.*

James Stordahl

1

WTH

As someone with a bipolar-2 anchor hanging on my neck, I need photos to remind me of stuff. Here I am outside the Iowa State Capitol, in downtown Des Moines. I believe we had four buses from Ankeny. This was the day that I decided to drive school bus on a regular basis.

The First Amendment

Congress shall make no law respecting an establishment of religion, or prohibiting the free exercise thereof; or abridging the freedom of speech, or the press, or the right of the people peaceably to assemble, and to petition the Government for a redress of grievances.

This new book is about a frame of mind. A view of the world. The way I perceive what I hear. Whether you see it as good or bad, the following paragraphs tell you what the world looks like, from my side of the road. A lot of my perceptions are a direct result of how I was value programmed. For some, it will be a little confusing. For a growing number of you it will sound like you are right at home.

My thought process for this book is the disintegration of the moral fiber in our country. The rise of hate groups. The foul language and actions in the streets. Where have all these wild-eyed, torch-bearing crazies come from?

I am horrified and deeply offended by the increasing number of stories about the rise (again) of racism—both at home and abroad.

President Trump's rhetoric and actions have empowered the likes of the neo-Nazis, the Ku Klux Klan and other white supremacists.

Political polarization, now at an all-time high and intensity, appears to feed on the hatred encouraged by the President and his staff.

The media has a professional obligation to expose this problem. Republicans must do what they haven't – speak out against the President, telling him there will be no more business as usual. Cowardice is no excuse for permitting unethical behavior.

Why have we become so isolated? What happened to thinking like a team, or as a community? Where did the checks-and-balances of knowing your neighbor go?

As a 22-year retired military veteran, I have experienced this type of general public behavior before. My other career, with the U.S. Postal Service, again introduced me to the overall attitude and

temperament that leads to this do-nothing
behavior. Or the more destructive – I don't
care behavior.

The phrase I keep coming up with is
KMA. The attitude that appears to be
prevalent in the way people treat each
other. I checked in with Google, and ended
up with the Urban Dictionary.

KMA means _Kiss My Ass_. _KMA_ is the abbreviation for _Kiss My Ass_.

It is commonly used in the business
world to refer to someone's last day of
work, either due to retirement or
resignation. In other words, "KMA" refers to
the day you can tell the people you work for
to kiss your ass, because they are no longer
your problem.

KMA also refers to a project that one
does for little or no pay ("I'll get to
these KMA projects after I finish my paying
work.") It has also been described as the
worst insult you could ever give anyone.
Ever.

There are growing 'pockets' of
followers, with the KMA attitude, in most
every corner of business and life. Many
times we laugh it off when we see it on TV,
in a situation comedy, where one of the
characters gives up and adopts the KMA
position. We see it in the growing incidents
of road rage, where combatants forget what

their reactions look like to other people.
KMA—I have been wronged!

We see it in the 40% of broken
relationships that ends in separation or
divorce. We experience it when the smug and
indifferent check-up person mindlessly bags
our groceries like a gorilla. It is rampant
in all branches of the military and totally
controls the workforce of the US Postal
Service.

The erratic and wild political scene
shows all the earmarks of a KMA attitude.
Who elected Trump? Where did these people go
to school? Did they go to school? How can
the Republicans in Congress and the Senate
show such disregard for the MAJORITY of
their constituents?

I recall being surprised, and amused,
when I first heard the reference in my early
years of the Postal Service. I actually
thought it was an active club, with fervent
members.

My initial reaction was that this was a
product of limited or poor education. The
results of years of living paycheck to
paycheck and being annoyed by anyone putting
on "airs".

It was, in fact, an inactive club — a
frame of mind taken by those that had given
up —welcome to the *Kiss My Ass (KMA)* club!

The explosion that resulted in the
disastrous 2016 election is playing out as a
New Civil War, only with numerous sides.
Some of the sides are not very big. Some of
the factions are slow to learn. Some groups
are violent. Maybe I will have to identify
them as orbits. Thought bubbles that roam
our airspace and will occasionally bump into
each other. It appears to me that a growing
number in my country have already identified
with the KMA syndrome.

It appears so obvious when politicians,

continue this practice even after they are caught on camera, or quoted in the paper.

I am from small orbit thinking. Small town, short Main Street thought process. For me, 1,700 people in my Minnesota hometown was the developing orbit. Short main street. Not unusual to have a tractor parked by the grocery store.

The Legion Club and VFW were always busy and the "gentlemen" parked in the alley when they picked up their 'hootch' at the only Municipal Liquor Store. Small paper bag, please.

My father was an Army infantry veteran of WWII. His proficiency with the rifle got him assigned as a sniper. He never talked about what he experienced. He never told us about the chunks of cement shrapnel imbedded in his back. He did not want surgery because he heard from 'somewhere' that he might be paralyzed from the surgery.

He never trusted the Veterans Administration (VA) hospitals. He was eligible for a number of things that he never asked for. He also never used any of the GI Bill, which could have helped him get additional education and/or training when he returned home. He felt all of those efforts were welfare, or handouts.

He was a prime candidate for PTSD, but never went any further than the Legion Club for therapy. Drinking and laughing with the 'boys' was all he desired, even while my brother and I were seated in the back seat of the car, in the alley, waiting for his therapy to be done. I guess that those were the first seeds of my own **KMA Syndrome**.

My own initial experiences with this way of thinking goes back more than 60 years. I am writing about this because, as a school bus driver, I can see the SAME mental health structure developing in kids in 2017. The easy way out…KMA.

In order to develop KMA, you must have a foundation laid in your brainpan. For many, it is the guidance from your mother. I believe that the naiveté for this small town kid was learning from a mother who was sternly raised by an alcoholic father and an enabling mother.

The grandfather I am talking about did not have an easy life. He was raised in a small house on the prairie, with four older sisters, trying to survive when their father went off to the big city to gamble and drink…sometimes for weeks. *I* was told

stories of my grandfather having to go hunt
and shoot rabbits for their supper.

Maybe it was the baseball line drive to
his head when he was a promising minor
league pitcher? Maybe it was falling off the
train during the winter, and landing on his
head? So, maybe that was one building block
for HIS drinking.

Maybe it was boxing matches with
Buffalo Bill Cody's grandson when they were
both in Army Boot Camp preparing for their
fun trip overseas for WWI? It could have
been the mustard gas attacks in France or
the poorly cooked rabbit stew they were
forced to eat, while in the trenches?

Whatever the reason, my mother was
value programmed in an alcoholic house.
There was no other way than to get along to
get along. Mom learned her lessons well. She
and Dad spawned four kids with a huge load
of problems. Depression was the biggest
hurdle. Compulsive behavior was next. Over-
eating, smoking, drinking – ignoring your
neighbors and discouraging having anyone
over to visit – I guess, the KMA Syndrome
was the least of her worries, following the
enabling of my Dad's drinking and 'silent
treatments'.

Just as I was thinking that my feelings
about the KMA state-of-mind was all mine, a
variety of news articles are appearing that
suggest that this is a far reaching malady.
What was once a civilized response, or a

measured reaction, now bursts through like a spoiled child—ranting about one side of the subject at hand.

As I write about this frame of mind, USA TODAY reminds us that our current President has displayed this attitude - in public - in print - on TV. When he was running for the office he decried special interests, but his allies are thriving.

Lobbying firms managed by former campaign aides, fundraisers and others with ties to President Trump and Vice President Pence have collected at least $28 million in federal lobbying fees since Trump assumed the presidency.

Leading the way: *Ballard Partners*, overseen by Brian Ballard, a veteran Florida lobbyist who raised money for Trump's campaign and inauguration.

Although Trump campaigned on a pledge to "drain the swamp" of Washington special interests, his former political aides and other figures in his orbit are building larger profiles in the world of influence he criticized.

In all, registered lobbyists with ties to Trump and Pence have leadership roles in at least 10 firms in Washington, a USA TODAY review shows. Other federal lobbyists with growing client lists and ties to the administration include Pence's former chief of staff Bill Smith, whose clients include AT&T; Victor Smith, who served as Pence's commerce secretary in Indiana; and Barry Bennett, a former Trump campaign aide who built a firm with a roster of domestic and deep-pocketed international clients.

Their lobbying is legal, and a spending surge is common when a new president enters the White House.

> *My question is: How did our Congress let this corruption flourish? Why is lobbying at this level legal?*

Here is a screenshot of four of my books, now on Amazon: Bipolar Dad; Bits & Pieces; Straggler, and Scatterbrain.

The Opinion page of the Des Moines Register is home to a variety guest columnists. For this chapter of my book, I choose to share the words of **John Hale.** John and his wife, Terri, own The Hale Group, an Ankeny-based consulting, advocacy and communication firm on aging and caregiving issues.

His article is titled,

"Welcome to Iowa, aka the Care Less State.

"A former Iowan now living out of state emailed me about a recent column I had written titled "Iowans Agree – Older Iowans Are Not a Priority."

Her question – "What's wrong with Iowa? Doesn't it care anymore?"

My answer: "It still cares, but it cares less."

The column highlighted then-recent news: that Iowa's Long-Term Care Ombudsman's Office, the office charged with the responsibility to protect the health, safety and rights of Iowans in nursing facilities, had told their eight regional staff that due to budget cuts, they could no longer travel to investigate complaints and advocate for residents and their families.

The travel stoppage sparked media attention across the state. Several print and television outlets commented on the cuts and made the case that action should be taken to get these ombudsmen back on the road to do the important work they are expected to do.

That hasn't happened. The ombudsmen are still tethered to their desks. Older Iowans and Iowans with disabilities are being poorly treated and inadequately served. To make matters worse, the staffing of the office is being gutted to further respond to the budget cuts. An office of 16 a few months ago is now down to 12. Recent losses, some by voluntary departures and some by position elimination and termination of employees, include:

- *The coordinator of volunteers across the state who visit nursing facilities and talk to residents about their concerns.*

- *The program manager who assisted Iowans with concerns about or disagreements with decisions made by the managed care organizations that administer the Medicaid program.*

- *The discharge specialist position that dealt with residents and facility management when a facility discharged a resident inappropriately, or when a facility closed.*

- *The legislative liaison for the office who addressed policy issues raised by the legislature and who provided the voice of Iowans in nursing facilities to elected leaders.*

2

Global warming

Never really liked dogs, until this one came along. A little Shi-Tzu/Bichon mix, nicknamed a 'Teddy Bear'… we call her 'Bailey'. When Charlotte was thinking of another pet, we went to a house in south Des Moines. I laid on the floor and one of the litter of five came over and licked my ear...we have enjoyed her since.

When you open up your *Thesaurus* (your what?), you will find many Don't care synonyms and Don't care Antonyms. I could have used any of these in my title, but I chose the tried and try often-used KMA phrasing that I grew up with in the US Postal Service.

<u>**Check out these Synonyms for don't care:**</u>

Neutral...unaffiliated..uninvolved

unattached...cut loose...don't care

fence-sitting...floating

free-spirited...

laid-back...middle ground...

middle of the road
nonaligned...nonpartisan...

on the fence...restrained..unpledged.

I am growing alarmed at the number of people I talk to, just don't care. A growing number do not even admit to watching and/or reading the news.

As a school bus driver, idea is tested often. I'll ask students if they read so-and-so in the paper – and the answer is NO. It appears that kids do not read the paper. They get their news from the internet, fake or real – that is how the news is flowing.

A recent newspaper headline: Tendency of scandals to grow can impact Trump presidency.

This may be true, but who does it impact?

Ron Ziegler, President Richard Nixon's press secretary, famously called the Watergate break-in a "third-rate burglary attempt" – and then it exploded into a wide-ranging scandal involving political dirty tricks, tax evasion, and obstruction of justice, ultimately forcing Nixon's resignation.

The Whitewater scandal dogged Bill Clinton for most of his presidency, as an investigation into an Arkansas real estate deal spun off into inquiries into the suicide of a White House lawyer, the firings at the White House Travel Office – and finally, Clinton's affair with intern Monica Lewinsky.

And now, President Trump finds himself in the midst of a series of controversies cascading like dominoes through the headlines.

What started as an investigation into Russian interference in the 2016 presidential election has morphed into as ever-expanding galaxy of scandals involving an adult-film star, influence peddling and – most recently – what the president knew about allegations of sexual abuse by the New York attorney general.

We have developed into a nation of tiny orbits. Each with their own thought process. Some are called Conservative. Some are caller Liberal. And that is just two bubbles among thousands that exist.

The break between the two major camps could be shown in anything printed or discussed when the subject "Global Warming" comes up.

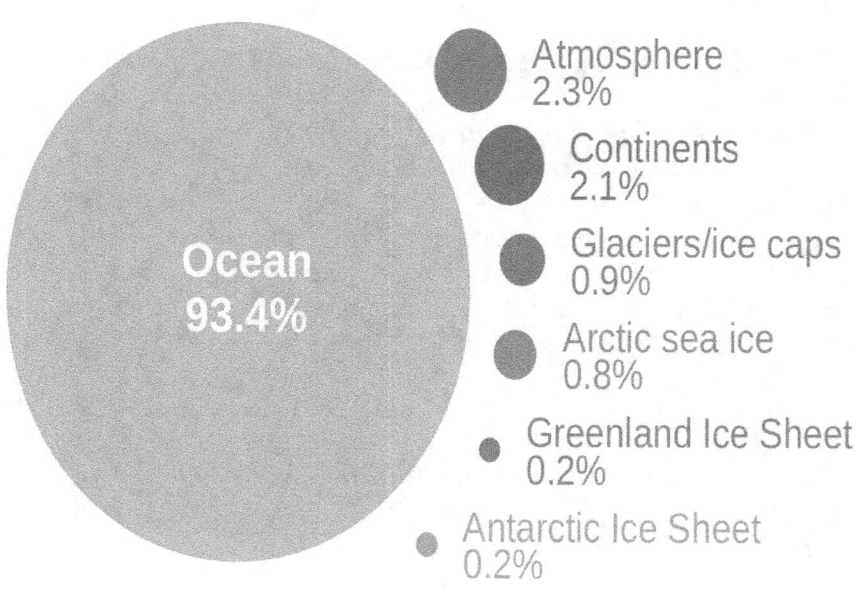

The Arctic is running a fever.

The magnitude and pace of the of the Arctic's sea-ice decline and ocean warming is "unprecedented" in at least the past 1,500 years and probably much longer, according to the National Oceanic and Atmospheric Administration.

The polar region shows no sign of returning to its reliably frozen state of recent decades, and its permafrost is thawing faster than ever before.

"The Arctic is going through the most unprecedented transition in human history, and we need better observations to understand and predict how these changes will affect everyone, not just the people of the north," said Jeremy Mathis, head of NOAA's Arctic Research Program. "The Arctic has traditionally been the refrigerator to the planet, but the door of the refrigerator has been left open."

Research shows that changes in Arctic sea ice and temperature can alter the jet stream, a major factor in U.S. weather and climate patterns.

"There are some connections between the warming in the Arctic and the extreme weather events down here," Mathis said.

The shift probably is partly responsible for the unusual weather in the

U.S. in recent years, including the destructive wildfires in California and the sharp cold snap in the South and East, said NOAA scientist James Overland.

Retired Navy rear admiral Timothy Gallaudet, acting NOAA administrator, said that "the rapid and dramatic changes we continue to see in the Arctic present major challenges and opportunities."

Let me pick one at random, one that I am immersed in on a daily basis. The education system. It used to be formal and organized. Now there are so many special interests picking it apart that it is hard to recognize. Decisions are made by committee and the result is unrecognizable, many times.

"Everybody is a genius. But if you judge a fish by its ability to climb a tree, it will live its whole life believing that it is stupid."

-Albert Einstein

In my central Iowa orbit, let's talk about a simple idea. The time to start school and the time to go home. Now, how could that be messed with?

Why are there a variety of times?

A recent Opinion in the Des Moines Register Editorial Page announced, "Schools wake up to teens' sleep needs." The Register said that Des Moines families should welcome proposal to change school hours.

They wrote:

Anyone who has been a teenager or raised one should appreciate a proposal to change school "bell times" in Des Moines. Officials are seeking to essentially flip the daily hours of elementary school with middle and high school, and the school board is expected to consider the idea.

The youngest students would start the day 45 to 75 minutes earlier in the morning and dismiss earlier in the afternoon. Older students would start 45 minutes later and dismiss later. High school would begin at 8:25 instead of the current tortuous-for-teens 7:40.

The new hours would go into effect next school year if the school board approves the plan.

It absolutely should. The change recognizes adolescent health research and the reality of contemporary families in which parents work outside the home.

Teenagers are nocturnal. Many spend evenings at a part-time job or participating in extracurricular activities. They get too little sleep, which is associated with health risks including being overweight, drinking alcohol and using drugs. High school seniors average less than 7 hours of sleep per night, although health experts say they need 8.5 to 9.5 hours.

Starting school later can help them get the shuteye they need, according to the

Centers for Disease Control and Prevention.
One study found delaying start times 30
minutes resulted in students actually going
to bed 18 minutes earlier, increasing their
sleep duration by about 45 minutes.

The additional snooze time can improve
teens' health and academic performance. An
added benefit: Later afternoon dismissal
means fewer unsupervised hours before
parents get home from work.

And starting elementary school earlier
could improve the lives and finances of
families. Working parents in Des Moines
frequently pay for Metro Kids Care in
elementary schools. The program allows them
to drop kids off early and get to work.
Starting classes at 7:30 could eliminate the
need for before-school care.

Here is a montage shots from daughter Betsy.

What is bipolar?

This is a good spot to enter more information on bipolar disorder. The previous montage of shots was gathered by daughter, Betsy. She has been struggling with bipolar disorder since she turned 14.

Bipolar Disorder is a treatable illness, marked by extreme changes in mood, thought, energy, and behavior. Bipolar disorder is also known as manic depression because a person's mood can alternate between the "poles"—mania (highs) and depression (lows). The change in mood can last for hours, days, weeks, or months.

Bipolar disorder is not a character flaw or sign of personal weakness.

Bipolar disorder affects more than 5.7 million adult Americans and 440,000 adult Canadians. It usually begins in late adolescence, often appearing as depression during teen years, although it can start in early childhood or later in life. Just this week I found out that one of our letter carriers started her bipolar journey midway through her 30's.

An equal number of men and women develop this illness. Men tend to begin with a manic episode, women with a depressive episode. Bipolar disorder is found among all ages, races, ethnic groups, and social classes. The illness tends to run in families and appears to have a genetic link.

Like depression and other serious illnesses, bipolar disorder can also negatively affect spouses, partners, family members, friends and co-workers.

My discovery was very slow and my acceptance was very erratic. I knew I saw life differently than most…and I had a hard time concentrating. Staying on task was impossible. Racing thoughts was an everyday occurrence. Our family therapy during Betsy's breakdown was the final straw that opened my eyes.

> *I found the attached subhead to this Opinion to be very enlightening.*

Much more to do in updating school schedule.

A change in school day start and end times is a promising sign that education officials are open to rethinking the traditional school schedule. And there is much to rethink. It does not make sense for 21st century families.

The vast majority of students aren't working in farm fields and milking cows. They do not need a "spring break" in the middle of March in chilly Iowa. Their education is not improved by a 10-week hiatus from classes in summer. Young people are unsupervised for hours while their parents work.

In Des Moines, schools dismiss students 90 minutes early every Wednesday. Over the course of a school year that robs young people of about 50 hours of instruction, more than a week of class. It disrupts daily schedules and inconveniences families.

With numerous "early outs" and days off throughout the year, it's hard for students to take school too seriously. Why not a longer school day? Why not a longer school year? A year-round schedule could improve learning, help kids retain information and accommodate working families.

My life-long mental state, that of being Bipolar-2, has given my the KMA attitude for most everything I get involved with. Relationships. Jobs. School.

Now that I am writing about it, this KMA frame of mind explains so much of my problem. Being "my own worst enemy" was one comment that landed early.

Bipolar has a simple definition. It means of two poles, as in polar opposite. Meaning two different places. Bipolar disease is a severe mood disorder that presents itself with both manic actions and thoughts and depression.

> ***Nearly 3 in 4 older Americans have two or more chronic health conditions, which often are diagnosed and treated by different doctors.***

According to the National Institute of Mental Health, 5.7 million people struggle with bipolar disorder, studies have found that 50% start showing signs before age 19. Betsy showed signs at age 14, I'm being told that 15-17 was my jumping off point. Bipolar disorder and depression continue to explode throughout the U.S. The resulting family disruptions, job losses and downgrades, and suicides SHOULD raise a red flag with someone!

There is no clear consensus as to how many types of bipolar disorder exist. The disease name gets thrown around TV and movies as some terrible, tragic event. The diagnosis appears to be a scary result of some very confused genes and chromosomes. Here are three definitions:

- **Bipolar I disorder** – A depressive or hypomanic episode is not required for diagnosis, but it frequently occurs.

- **Bipolar II disorder** – <u>(This appears to be my domain)</u> – No manic episodes, but one or more hypomanic episodes and one or more major depressive episode.

Once you get over the 'stage fright' of appearing on camera, then the rest is fun. In truth, I don't think I ever had stage fright. Being on stage, or on camera was always a "rush" for me. Only the Bipolar Gods can tell why I did not pursue this passion with more vigor. What was I afraid of? Moving? Abandonment of the 'comfortable' small-town life that I knew?

You get to meet lots of new people. Many of them have regular jobs and are in it for the first time. Some are 'junkies' that have stood in line before and like getting the little 'fix' that acting can do for you. Since the movies starting being made in Iowa, in 2008, I have been increasingly active in independent films, as well as local commercials. Mostly background business, but very satisfying. I am averaging one on-camera experience every 4-6 months. In August 2018, I worked two days on the set of the new promotional ad for Wild Rose Casino, in Jefferson, IA. Earlier, in June, I appeared on the new promotional piece fcr Iowa Public TV. At that same time I posed on a park bench with my partner, for a dramatic photo for a national promotion for LGBTQ events.

My first dysfunctional depression hit when I was around 10 years old. It followed an episode where I was being teased. I think it was by a girl. Does not make that much difference now, because teasing and the inability to handle it has been one of my great weaknesses.

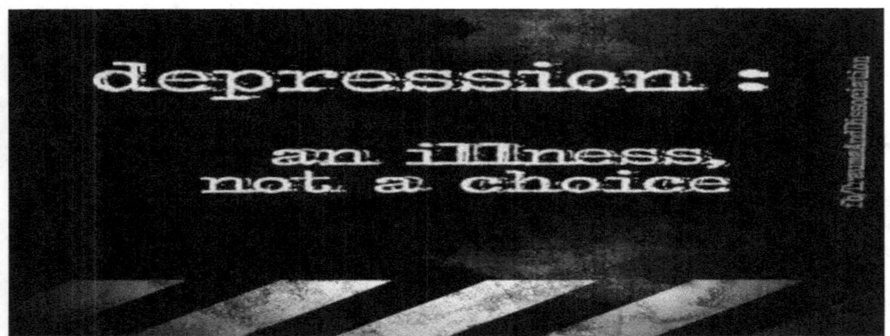

It has been 50 years since that first recalled depression and I have finally been diagnosed with bipolar illness. I feel grateful for this discovery because I finally have a reason for my irrational, manic behavior. I now know why I have been labeled as "My own worst enemy". Too much effort to be accepted, too much talk to get my point across, too many altered views of ways to get things done.

An analytical brain.

Do your homework, get the facts. Bipolar sufferers don't have time for homework!

My sad story is within my head every day. Through extensive therapy I can recall awkward reactions to a number of life's situations. Embarrassments. Teasing. Bonehead ideas. Knucklehead reactions. Nonchalant responses to situations that demanded better. Erratic behavior never challenged. A secretive approach developed to deal with everything. No important discussions at home. A very distant father who never discussed serious matters.

Is it hereditary? Is it just me? Now it makes no difference. I just have to continue to understand and learn more about this irritating, debilitating disease. Getting the diagnosis is scary. Getting your head wrapped around the 'fuzzy' way you deal with

life is like watching a movie with someone
doing wrong things in their life. My
hindsight is clear. Only problem is that I
am reliving stupid comments and sad
reactions that could have turned out
differently. I've got a long list of do-
overs!

> **Researchers at the University of Essex
> found that 94% of those who exercised
> -walking, running, cycling, gardening
> --saw mental health benefits.**
>
> **Arianna Huffington**

3

GETTING BY

When I titled this chapter, "Getting By", I started to think about the many kids now being pushed through school with very little common sense and/or discipline. What are we going to do with all of those entitled and 'lost' kids when they stumble into the workforce?

When you Google a variety of questions about kids behavior, you will get an amazing amount of feedback. First up is a response from TODAY.com.

<u>**Ruth A, Peters, Ph.D., wrote in TODAY:**</u>

Law #5: Connect Consequences to Behavior

I guarantee you can get better behavior from your child. But there is only one way to do it. You must make it perfectly, unmistakably clear that what he does will determine what happens to him. No amount of nudging, cajoling, or, worst of all, threatening, will do a lick of good until you connect consequences to his behavior.

Psychologists have long struggled with the chicken-and-egg concept of what comes first – attitudinal or behavioral change. One group believes that folks must adjust their perceptions or feelings before they will change their actions. The other camp campaigns for motivating behavioral change first, with changes in desires, perceptions and feelings following.

An article in the Des Moines Register, written by a student at Iowa State University, has shown me a new path. The writer is ***Alex Felker*** (arfelker@iastate.edu) and he very cleverly laid out an idea for getting classroom behavior back in line. I kind of like it. My experience as a school bus driver has taught me that each year weakens the fiber that used to guide the students.

<u>Here are some excerpts:</u>

"**Corporal** punishment is out; the nation has spoken and the paddle is going the way of the dunce cap (though 19 states still allow paddling). Academic discipline—detentions, suspensions, expulsions—are a useful tool, but equally dangerous; Des Moines area school leaders have already drastically cut back on their use of such methods amidst growing disparities along racial lines."

"**So** we can't beat good behavior into students, and we are limited in our ability to tell them to scram. What else is left?"

"**To** me, the answer is clear: We must embarrass them into submission."

"**It** is not difficult to humiliate the average 15-year-old. If fact, under any usual circumstance one has to make an exhaustive effort not to.

"**So** this is my scheme: a peer-pressure taught humility. A created atmosphere of reasonable expectation—built upon the kind of healthy fear—that must be cultivated for a proper educational environment: Mutual respect.

"**Ironically,** it is in the teacher's readiness to embarrass the student that we

see the respect. This is because he expects
better of them. He expects them to act as
adults, and, in doing so, affords them the
congruent respect. This is the kind of
necessary mutual respect that is required
for meaningful learning.

"**Unfortunately,** there is one obvious
flaw to my system: It requires generally
intelligent and competent teachers; who, as
a cohort, are in such short supply and paid
such ma little amount that those worth their
salt tend to be driven provisionally insane
after a few years in the classroom."

---

*Just as this (above) was written, all of the
West Virginia teachers were out on strike
for 9 days, due to very low wages. The
average West Virginia teacher was making
$45,000 annually. They finally got the
statehouse to listen and they won a 5% pay
raise. Now Arizona is thinking of taking the
same drastic action.*

When did this country decide to give up
on hopeful thinking? When did it start to
become apparent that a larger majority of
this country just slipped into the despair
of realizing that most people do not care?

The lost feeling of never being able to
amount to much can be a giant drag on your
mental health. You can see it where you
shop. You can see it in the playgrounds. You
can see it on the open road.

Des Moines Register columnist Kim

Norvell recently wrote: "Iowa's suicide rate increased over 35 percent in 17 years".

She wrote: Iowa's suicide rate has increased faster than most states' over the pst two decades, according to new data from the Centers for Disease Control.

Every state but Nevada has seen a rise in deaths by suicide between 1999 and 2016. Iowa saw a 36.2 percent increase during that time; 17 states had a higher rate.

"I'm sad, but I'm not shocked," said Ryan Nesbit, co-chair of the American Foundation for Suicide Prevention's Iowa Chapter. "I fear numbers will continue to rise in Iowa and the whole country."

He attributes the increase to a lack of options for Iowans with mental illness. At least eight Iowa hospitals have closed inpatient psychiatric units in recent years, including state mental hospitals in Mount Pleasant and Clarinda.

The state also has a lack of qualified physicians who can treat mental illness. There are only 123 doctors, 122 nurse practitioners and 33 physicians assistants who practice psychiatry, according to data from the National Alliance on Mental Illness Greater Des Moines.

And nearly two-thirds of Iowa's 99 counties lack a practicing psychiatrist in the county, the organization found.

Gov. Kim Reynolds recently signed a sweeping mental-health bill, providing funding for six regional "access centers"

for people who need care but don't require
full hospitalization. It also requires
suicide prevention training for school
employees.

> **"Many people who should seek help
> don't. We as a society have to
> get over that stigma."**
>
> *-Ryan Nesbit*
>
> *Co-chair of the American Foundation for Suicide
> Prevention Iowa Chapter*

"We've had some good steps in the last
year, but we have so far to go," said Teresa
Bomhoff, president of the National Alliance
on Mental Illness Greater Des Moines. "Does
it offer a promise for the future?
Absolutely. But the proof will always be
whether we have the funds of the workforce
to carry it all the way through."

The CDC found in its study that more
than half of people who died by suicide did
not have a diagnosed mental health
condition.

"Many people who should seek help
don't," Nesbitt said. "We as a society have
to get over the stigma."

The CDC found relationship problems or
loss, substance misuse, physical health
problems and job, money, legal or housing
stress often contributed to death by suicide
nationwide.

It's difficult to pinpoint why 433 Iowans who died by suicide last year decided to end their lives, said Pat McGovern, data manager and suicide prevention coordinator with the Iowa Department of Mental Health.

"Suicide is very complex, and so many factors do play a role in that," he said.

The state is using a new reporting tool to collect "actionable information" on Iowans who die by suicide, including their age, race, means of death and mental health history to determine how to direct resources that will make the most impact, he said.

How to help someone who is suicidal

- Be direct. Talk openly and matter-of-factly about suicide.

- Be willing to listen. Allow expressions of feelings. Accept the feelings.

- Be non-judgmental. Don't debate whether suicide is right or wrong, or whether feelings are good or bad. Don't lecture on the value of life.

- Get involved. Become available. Show interest and support.

- Don't dare him or her to do it.

- Don't act shocked. This will put distance between you.

- Take action. Remove means, such as firearms or stockpiled pills.

Suicide in Iowa

According to the American Foundation for Suicide Prevention, in Iowa:

- Six times as many people die by suicide per year than by homicide.

- One person dies by suicide every 20 hours in the state.

- Suicide is the ninth leading cause of death overall, but second among Iowans ages 15-34 years old.

- The CDC found 47.2 percent of Iowans who died by suicide used a firearm.

- Men are more likely to die by suicide than women.

While stitching a cut on the hand of a 75 year old farmer, whose hand was caught in the squeeze gate while working cattle, the doctor struck up a conversation with the old man.

Eventually the topic got around to politicians and their role as leaders.

The old farmer said, "Well, as I see

it, most politicians are 'Post turtles'."

Not being familiar with the term, the doctor asked him what a 'post turtle' was.

The old rancher said, "When you're driving down a country road and you come across fence post with a turtle balanced on top, that's a post turtle."

The old farmer saw the puzzled look on the doctor's face so he continued to explain. "You know he didn't get up there by himself, he doesn't belong up there, he doesn't know what to do while he's up there, he's elevated beyond his ability to function, and you wonder what kind of a dumb ass put him up there to begin with."

Best explanation of a politician I've heard of.

Des Moines Register Letter to the Editor

"On May 19, 2017, Scott Michael Greene pleaded guilty to the murders of two local police officers, Des Moines Sgt. Anthony Beminio and Urbandale Officer Justin Martin. While I agree that Greene should pay for his actions, I wonder if this crime would have happened if more mental health institutes has still been available in Iowa."

"Where are the facilities for people who are incapable of living in reality,

people who act out to stop the madness? The proper facilities could allow them to get regulated on their medications, facilities that could house them and protect them from themselves and others. Iowa has failed its job of taking care of those who are incapable of taking care of themselves. Iowa has allowed the mentally disturbed to be on the streets, in the homeless camps or terrorizing their relatives."

"Greene is an example of how Iowa is taking care of its mentally ill people. It is putting them in jail. Does it take such horrendous acts for Iowa's lawmakers to take another look at helping our mentally ill residents?"

--Lorraine Riseley, Des Moines

Here I go with one my pet peeves.

Handling school children with kid gloves.
Lack of discipline throughout our education
has caused all sorts of problems that are
showing up across the board.

My local paper, the *Des Moines Register*
recently printed an opinion on the subject.
The headline: Schools don't need another
mandate – How about requiring every student
to be educated?

Excerpts are as follows:

"**Most** Iowans have ideas they think are
good. But, if you're one of the 150 Iowans
who is also a state lawmaker, you have the
ability to try to codify those ideas in Iowa
Code.

Some of the proposals from these
individuals need rethinking.

One recent example is House Study Bill
573, sponsored by Rep. Walt Rogers. This
three-page nugget would impose a redundant
mandate on Iowa schools. The Cedar Falls
Republican wants to require students to
correctly answer 60 percent of questions on
a civics exam to receive a high school
diploma.

This is the same test given by the U.S.
Citizenship and Immigration Services and the
same percentage required by immigrants who
want to become citizens. Rogers not only
thinks students should have to pass it, but
also wants to allow them to start trying in

seventh grade.

As if schools don't have enough tests to administer already. As it there's any extra state money to cover the cost of such a mandate. As if this should be the educational priority when an estimated 10,000 Iowa third-graders cannot read at grade level. The only lobbyists registered in support of the bill are from an organization called the "Civics Proficiency Institute," and Arizona organization.

Yet Rogers insists it's "common sense that kids today should have an understanding of basic U.S. civics."

We agree. Perhaps that's why Iowa lawmakers recognized this decades ago. State Law already mandates that every school or school district require students to take U.S. government to graduate.

That's in addition to the legislatively imposed American history graduation requirement. And the four years of English, three years of math, three years of science and three years of social science. It is in addition to the mandate from lawmakers that students take "one-eighth" of physical education in each semester of high school – unless a parent secures a religious exemption from P.E.

What other graduation requirements and federal tests would lawmakers seek to require for a high school diploma? Why stop at treating Iowa teenagers like immigrants seeking citizenship? Perhaps students correctly answer 70 percent of questions of

a civil service exam taken by some
government employees or pass the basic
physical fitness test for the U.S. Army,
which includes
a 2-mile run.

The
Registers'
first thought
when hearing
about this
legislation was
that Iowa
lawmakers
should be
required to
pass the civics
test to
continue
serving in the
Legislature.
They could
sharpen their pencils and gather at the
Statehouse on a Friday to sit for the exam,
with their answer and scores immediately
made available to voters.

Our second thought was that Rogers and
other lawmakers should put the brakes on
dictating what students should learn until
they require all students to actually
receive an education in this state.

The Iowa Legislature has so far refused
to repeal Independent Private Instruction.
This relatively new option in homeschooling
allows parents to keep children home, notify
no one, and teach kids nothing, let alone
anything about civics. These parents are
allowed to disregard every current state

education law and could disregard the one Rogers wants to add to Iowa Code. Doing away with this dangerous, irresponsible option is well, common sense.

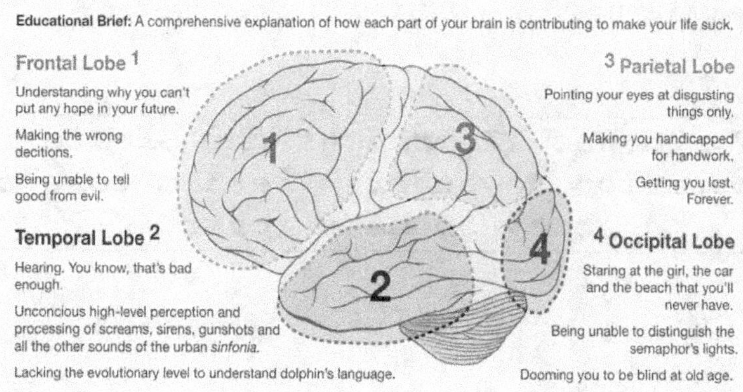

The mental health system in Iowa is broken. The previous Governor (Branstad) gutted the system – like his other criminal Republican Governor cohorts. After years of complaints and crises, Branstads' replacement, Kim Reynolds, is not doing much better. She finally had to confront the state's growing problem of incarcerating mentally ill patients. No hospital rooms means they go to jail.

In March, 2018, Gov. Reynolds signed into law a bill that allows magistrates to hold mental-health commitment hearings by video-conferencing instead of in person.

Iowa sheriff's deputies routinely drive hours to retrieve local residents from faraway hospitals, where the patients are being treated because local psychiatric units are full.

The deputies pick up the patients and drive them back to their home counties for court hearings to determine if they need to be committed for continued treatment.

World War II brought the Greatest Generation together. Vietnam tore the baby boomers apart.

4

Rays of sunshine

Grandpa and Grandma Stordahl with five grandkids, two years ago. We now have two more.

If people don't read, they develop no history. When people rely on their close friends for reliable information, who's to say it is reliable?

The headlines in the Sioux City Journal read, *"Schools review safety plans"*.

What else can they say? The review is pushed by the most recent mass shooting – the one in Parkland, Florida. Another mass killing of unprotected students!

According to the Journal, measures include cameras, mock drills and social media tools. Really? And the money will come from where?

Here are excerpts from Journal reporter Bret Hayworth (bhayworth@siouxcityjournal.com).

Metro Sioux City school administrators say they have detailed security plans in place that aim to prevent mass shootings like the one that killed 17 in Florida.

In the wake of the second deadliest shooting as a U.S. school, locals say they have no current plans to install metal detectors at entrances but are contemplating additional safety measures.

School district officials said they are mindful of keeping security plans fresh to try to have the safest schools possible. The Catholic schools and Sioux City and South

Sioux City public school districts hold training drills at least once a year to make sure students and staff know what to do in various crises situations.

Can you tell if this was an abusive family? Check out what happens when the "Silent Treatment" is employed as an active arm of discipline in the house. In this case, when the father passed, the family fell apart due to distinct variations of how the kids were 'value programmed' and how they responded to the adopted their own silent treatments.

5

Darkness

Quote:

"A person who sees moral equivalence in Charlottesville, who talks about and treats women like they're pieces of meat, who lies constantly about matters big and small and insists the American people believe it – that person's not fit to be President of the United States, on moral grounds."

- Former FBI Director James Comey

Darkness is one way to describe my feelings about the world we live in. Adrift with no collective moral goalpost. Road rage is the go-to mentality in today's busy streets. I see it every day as I drive my school bus. Cars will speed up to reclaim their space if someone turns off or slows down.

Many times I sense that the oncoming car will not hit the brakes, when they can speed up to take their space back. What has happened to our compassion? Where is out patience? Is it the constant drumbeat of negativity?

Is it the constant spray of news where disrespect is acknowledged and many times rewarded.

As I look at a recently saved headline, in my stack of newspapers of worth, I am so sad to see the headline: "The smell of death still fills Mosul."

Remember the politician that did not understand a question at last year's political circus. He did not know what Mosul was. (It was a beautiful city, on the Tigris River, the second largest city in Iraq).

It has been nearly a year since the Iraqi Prime Minister declared this war-devastated city liberated from the Islamic State.

And the putrid odor still fills the air from the thousands of corpses left in the rubble.

I mean, talk about not caring, turning your back on fellow man. Showing the KMA attitude on a grand scale.

The bodies of civilians and Islamic State militants can now be found throughout Mosul, once Iraq's second-largest city, abandoned in bombed-out buildings, tossed in roadside rubbish heaps or discarded in and around the Tigris River.

My own pet peeve is the terrible darkness that covers the mental health aspect of our country. There is a real **KMA attitude** when it comes to getting help...because there is very little help, **IF** you can even find a source.

How many times do you try? How many times should you continue to pound your head into a wall?

Access to acute care mental health care beds saves lives. Unfortunately, Iowa's mental health care system is missing key components that negatively impact access to services. (This revelation was exposed in the Des Moines Register, 2-28-2018, in the article "Pieces missing for mental health care in Iowa."

Among the missing components is the effective treatment of a small percentage of the population who suffer from a persistent serious mental illness.

These Iowans require special consideration as their lives are severely impacted by these diseases and their use of services and cost of treatment are disproportionally high.

Effective treatment for these individuals does three things:

1. Improves their quality of life.

2. Improves access to acute care psychiatric beds.

3. Reduces the overall operating costs for Iowa's mental health care system.

The Treatment Advocacy Center has been sounding the alarm about the lack of state-operated acute care psychiatric beds in Iowa for several years (currently 96 MHI beds). Fifty-seven percent of Iowa's prison population suffers from either a serious mental illness or has a chronic mental health diagnosis.

These numbers are staggeringly high and many of these forensic patients are in the two remaining Iowa MHIs.

Iowa's availability of acute care beds is at a crises level, but how many additional beds are needed? The answer is not as simple as adding some arbitrary number of beds distributed across Iowa hospitals (which currently house 615 beds).

The total count of staffed acute psychiatric beds in Iowa is more than 700.

That's 23.3 beds per 100,000 Iowa residents. The Treatment Advocacy Center recommends having 50 state-operated acute care psychiatric beds per 100,000 residents – twice the total number of acute care beds in Iowa.

There are a number of ways that darkness can overcome us. The knowledge that a growing number of our fellow Americans do not give a crap about the outcome of their actions is a dangerous sign for our country.

One was that the KMA attitude can take hold is the constant struggle to make ends meet. Pay the bills. Maybe have a little fun, like all those smiling faces on TV and in the movies.

<u>A study posted in USA TODAY tells us:</u>

Being broke saps mental bandwidth

Writer Dan Vergano writes: Just being broke, in and of itself, damages abilities to make good decisions in a way roughly equivalent to losing 13 IQ points – or constantly losing a night's sleep.

Performed in New Jersey and among sugar cane farmers in India, the experiments suggest that the mental bandwidth taken up with worries about being strapped explain the poor decision making widely seen among low-income families.

That includes taking costly payday loans to missing appointments.

Rather than the poor being poor because they make bad decisions, they make bad decisions because they are poor.

"You and I would suffer the same way if we were broke," says study author Eldar Shafir of Princeton University.

"It's not just abject poverty. Once your budget is constrained, your decision making suffers."

In the experiments reported in the journal Science, Shafir and his colleagues first tested 336 shoppers at a New Jersey mall, people with an average household income of $74,000. They were presented with financial problems such as deciding how to pay for hypothetical car repairs.

Faced with easy $150 car repairs, rich and poor alike made good decisions on whether to forgo the repairs, pay in full or take loans with varied, sometimes heavy, interest rates to pay for the repairs.

The rich also performed well on weighing how to deal with $1,500 repairs, but the poor did significantly worse, more often taking out onerous loans to immediately pay for repairs instead of longer-term ones with better rates.

Looking to rule out cultural or seasonal explanations for the effect, the team next carried out similar experiments on 464 sugar cane farmers from 54 villages in the Tamil Nadu region of India.

These small farmers are paid once yearly at varied times at varied times around the year for their harvest. The researchers tested them when they had just been paid, and were flush, and when they were two months from their next payday, and broke.

"Simply put, being poor taps out one's mental reserves," says University of Minnesota psychologist Kathleen Vohs, in a commentary on what she calls the "eye-opening" study.

"These findings suggest that decisions requiring many trade-offs, which are common in poverty, render subsequent decisions prone tc favoring impulsive, intuitive, and often regrettable options."

Shafir acknowledges the study results contrast with "pick yourself up by your own bootstraps" thinking about escaping poverty.

"We only have so much bandwidth to make decisions and if yours is taken up daily with child care and getting to work on time when your boss yelled at you yesterday, you won't make good decisions," he says.

This study confirms my thoughts about successful politicians. They always promise a better tomorrow.

Like our current President, catering to the uneducated and the under achievers. Promise them something better and they will vote for you. Do whatever you can to convince the electorate that a better day is coming and they will put you in charge. Do whatever you can and say whatever it takes to take their minds off of their position in life and they will make you President. Sad.

"Loose lips sink ships."

A very clever war-time reminder to keep your yap shut. During WWII, that slogan was part of a U.S. anti-espionage campaign. It employed iconic, colorful posters with slogans aimed at preventing American intelligence from falling into the enemies' clutches.

Today, with all the talk of Russia waging cyber-warfare on American elections, we need a new campaign. Democracy dies when you share lies. Know it's true before you tweet.

The real national scandal isn't whether Donald Trump's campaign colluded with the Russian propaganda campaign to influence the

2016 election. If that happened, it's terrible and it must never happen again.

But the real scandal is that we, the American people, cooperated with such spectacular enthusiasm to aid the Russians in spreading lies and distortion.

Twitter is January disclosed that it had discovered more than 50,000 Russia-linked accounts that posted automated material about the 2016 election.

The company said it sent notices to 1.4 million.

The stigma of being mentally ill is darkness. Being afraid to let other people know that you suffer from some form of mental illness can cast a cover of darkness over your entire life.

Late in 2017, the Des Moines Register and Des Moines University held a Forum on Mental Illness, on the DMU campus. Register reporter Kathie Obradovich was the moderator and 12 candidates for governor attended.

Following are excerpts from an opinion voiced in the Register by candidate Jake Porter.

"On Dec. 5, I was one of 12 candidates for governor present at the Des Moines Register-sponsored gubernatorial forum on mental health."

"We were asked what the most pressing problem in Iowa's mental health system was, and what we do as governor to fix it. My answer, based on personal experience, was simple. We must first address the stigma surrounding mental illness. To lead, I would have to reveal my own experience."

"In 2011, I contemplated suicide. I was going to do it. I was going to end my own life."

"One afternoon, I went for a long drive. The question was not if, but how I was going to do it. Near the end of my drive, I had a profound spiritual experience. Many people have had these thoughts, but sadly, not come back from them. They left their friends and family behind. In Iowa, suicide is the second leading cause of death for people my age (15-34). Suicide and mental illness are issues that impact us all, at some level."

"Before the forum, I had told only a handful of people about my experience. In fact, for years it frightened me to think, let alone talk, about how I came that close to ending it all. What would other people think? Would they reject me for jobs if they knew? What would family and friends think? Would people disassociate from me?"

"I didn't plan to make such an admission. When the question was asked about the most important factor surrounding mental health, there was only one answer I felt was right. We must address the stigma surrounding mental illness. If I can't talk about something personal like that, there is certainly a stigma surrounding it. If this is true for me, I am sure it must be true for others."

"Dr. Andy McQuire, a fellow candidate for Iowa governor, made a great point. If someone would have walked into the room with a broken arm *or leg, we would all go over and help them. If they were addicted to drugs, would we do the same? What if they were suffering from a mental illness?"*

*"I am certainly not the first Iowa politician to contemplate suicide and later talk about it. Former Gov. Harold Hughes contemplated suicide during a long battle with alcohol addiction following Worl War II and before he became governor of Iowa and a U.S. Senator. He also wrote a book titled **"The Man From Ida Grove"** that discusses it in great detail."*

"If you are depressed, suicidal or addicted to alcohol or illegal or legal drugs, it is nothing to be ashamed of or embarrassed by. I know people who have recovered from methamphetamine addiction, alcohol addiction and suicide attempts. It is perfectly acceptable to admit that you have a problem or are struggling and ask for help. The stigma can stay around only as long as we ignore the problems. I just wish I had known this almost eight years ago."

Jake Porter is a business consultant in Council Bluffs and is a Libertarian Party candidate for governor.

Just like the sun following the moon, from light to dark, so goes the conversations and the headlines in today's papers.

For those of us, the shrinking-thinking generation, the stories and headlines are getting very heavy and very dark.

One of my favorite columnists is Leonard Pitts, writing for the Miami Herald. Following are excerpts from his recent column in the Des Moines Register.

Today's politics proof that tyranny could happen here.

What if Donald Trump were smart?

It is likely not a question you've given a lot of thought. After all, the urgency of our ongoing disaster leaves little time for speculation, One is too busy tallying up the damage that's happening now to worry about the damage that could.

But maybe it's time we did.

Trump's presidency has forced us to see our vulnerability to new media manipulation and disinformation. Truth can be whatever you need it to be.

It is not far-fetched to wonder if Trump is not simply writing the playbook, showing the next president how easily a stable democracy can be subverted.

© 2009 FreeSpeechStickers.com

So, as we grapple with the daily outrages of this presidency, it would be smart to begin inoculating future generations against one that could be worse. Now would be an excellent time to push even harder for internet giants like Facebook and Twitter to find better ways of purging their platforms of false news and hate.

Now would also be an excellent time for schools to beef up their teaching of philosophy, history, civics and social studies. Teach those things as a means of helping people think critically, value truth and internalize the ideals that are supposed to make America America.

The hope—in the end, the only real hope we have—is that people who do all that will be less susceptible to toxic ideologies.

Consider that, even lacking a real ideology, toxic or otherwise, Trump has already inflicted damage. It is hardly incidental that the New York City Anti-Violence Project just reported that 2017 saw an 86 percent spike in hate crime killings of LGBTQ people.

Or that the FBI arrested a Michigan man after he allegedly threaten to murder CNN reporters for reporting, as Trump calls it, "fake news." Or that the Pew Research Center found that the percentage of nations expressing confidence in in America sank from 64% to 22% in the first five months of the Trump regime.

Or that the percentage of Americans expressing confidence in their government has dropped 14 percentage points to just 33% over the last year.

*Speaking for myself, Trump has made watching
the nightly news a grueling experience. I am
sick of seeing his face and sick of hearing
his voice. He is so far out of touch with
the majority that I am sleepless at night
with fear of his next stupid move. And how
did a cretin like that Steve Miller ever get
so close to the Oval Office. Miller looks
like a back ground "extra" in a WWII
movie...and he is not with the good guys!*

Here is an example: His support for Roy Moore in the special election in Alabama. My favorite columnist, from the Des Moines Register, Rekha Basu, picked this candidacy apart and I applaud her for her in-depth dissection of a very evil man.

Following are excerpts from her Opinion column:

How can people of faith support Moore?

What Senate candidate is accused of defies basic principles of morality, decency and lawfulness.

"The Alabama state auditor's website says this about its current occupant "Jim Zeigler was led to Christ and baptized by Pastor William K. Weaver." I'm not sure how the state auditor's religious affiliation is relevant to his role as a public official, but clearly it's something the Republican

Ziegler believes his constituents care about."

"Zeigler marched with Roy Moore's anti-gay defenders last year in support of the then-state Supreme Court chief justice, who had defied a U.S. Supreme Court order to recognize same-sex marriage. Moore was charged with violating judicial ethics and disobeying the law. But some of the faithful, including Zeigler, suggested they were answering to God rather than the man-made laws.

"**As** one marcher told the Birmingham News, "Every stand I've ever seen him (Moore) take in these 15 years has been clearly based on God's word and God's law."

"**If** so, you'd expect that when allegations surfaced of Moore sexually preying on girls as young as 14 when he was district attorney, such supporters would be up in arms. But not Zeigler. He used the Biblical story of Joseph and Mary in Moore's defense, suggesting the late 1970s and early "80s were true, well, "Mary was a teenager and Joseph was an adult carpenter."

That was too much for evangelist commentator Ed Stetzer, who wrote in Christianity Today, "If this is evangelism, I'm on the wrong team. But it is not. Christians don't use Joseph and Mary to explain child molesting accusations."

Moore's younger brother, Jerry, does. He compared his brother to Jesus Christ in being unfairly persecuted. Alabama state Rep. Ed Henry said, "If they believe this

man is predatory, they are guilty . I think
someone should prosecute and go after them."

Alabama Secretary of State John Merrill
initially said he was satisfied when Moore
said he didn't do it. But Merrill himself
has admitted to having an affair while
married with a woman who was the wife of a
friend of his, after the friend told him she
was having an affair and sought his help.
When reports of that surfaced in 2015, he
defended himself by saying the woman was the
aggressor.

Merrill has since modified his stance
on Moore to repeat the line of White House
officials: If the accusations are true,
Moore should get out of the race. But they
haven't specified how that truth should be
determined.

6

Thoughts and prayers

Such a trite and overused phrase. You
hear it at every funeral. You hear it from
every politician. It does have a soft touch
to it, but it means nothing to most. I mean,
"When do you EVER share your thoughts and

prayers?"

It is almost like an apology. Like, I did not care in life, but now I toss a little sympathy your way. So that way I will be able to feel a little more human.

I am thinking that this country had better start loading up all their thoughts and prayers as we quickly descend into the crapper. The political garbage floating around is enough to gag a person. Lies after lies. All the way to the top. Many times starting at the top.

Dictionary:

Use*ful id*i*ot

/yoosfel ideat/

"The phrase 'useful idiots,' often attributed to an earlier Vladimir, <u>referred to Westerners who had been successfully manipulated by Soviet propaganda.</u>"

Former NSA and CIA Director Michael Hayden revels Jade Helm was Russian Disinformation Campaign

Austin, TX – Former NSA and CIA Director Michael Hayden revealed that Jade Helm 15 was a test-run of the first Russian disinformation campaign.

Russia engaged in information warfare to convince Texans that Jade Helm 15 was an Obama planned military exercise to round up political dissidents.

The story drew massive controversy as Texas Governor Abbott lent credence to conspiracy theorists by calling in the Texas National Guard to monitor our own U.S. Military.

Why is this significant?

- In 2015, Texas Republican Gov. Greg Abbott called up the Texas National Guard to monitor federal military exercises, a move that questioned the integrity of our troops and fed the conspiracy theories that President Barack Obama was setting up an invasion of Texas.

- Hayden's revelations now make it clear that Abbott was a Russian pawn.

- After the success Russians had regarding Jade Helm, they made the decision to play in the electoral process in 2016.

Texas Democratic Party Deputy Executive Director Manny Garcia issued the following statement:

"Republican Gov. Greg Abbott was a Russian pawn and a useful idiot for Russian efforts to turn gullible Texas Republicans against the United States.

Just when I started to think the world would settle down and really take school killings seriously, writer Christal Hayes authored an article in USA Today.

"Copycat threats fuel the fear"

Breathless and whispering through the phone, a 13-year old student called for help from her Ohio high school. "Help," she said in between whimpers. "He's got a gun. He's got the gun in my mouth."

Anxiety was already running high: It had been only a week after the deadly

shooting in Parkland, Fla. Police
dispatchers then got three other calls from
Withrow University High School in
Cincinnati. But it was all a hoax.

It's a stunt that other teens and kids
across the nation have pulled after
tragedies, creating fear in communities and
bringing costly investigations by police and
federal agents who have no choice but to
take the threats with deadly seriousness.
After the school shooting in Parkland, Fla.,
638 copycat threats were reported from Feb.
15 to Feb. 27.

The rise of threats after a high-
profile mass killing is nothing new. But the
incidents are hard to quantify, because they
are not tracked nationally by any government
agency.

A review by USA TODAY of published
accounts, however, paints a picture of a
growing problem that is no joke.

More than 130 threats were reported and
analyzed by the USA TODAY NETWORK in the
nine-day span after the Valentine's Day high
school shooting in Parkland, Fla., that left
17 dead. Also, non-profits such as the
Educator's School Safety Network have
compiled a list of threats using media
reports. The group found that the jarring
638 threats targeted schools in the two
weeks after the Parkland shootings, a number
they say is probably on the low side.

The dramatic increase in threats – from 10 to about 70 a day – has left school administrators and authorities walking a fine line in dealing with a threat's credibility.

At the root of the problem, experts say, are students who are too young to realize the severity of their acts.

"There are usually two common traits in these individuals," said Mary Ellen O'Toole, a former FBI profiler. "They're young, and their judgment is poor. I mean, a brain isn't really formed until your early 20s."

Texas, with 55 reports, had the most since the shooting. Next in line are Ohio, California, Florida and Pennsylvania, according to data from the Educator's School Safety Network, which tracks such incidents and trains schools on how to handle them.

Some threats were real, and law enforcement was able to thwart the plot, but the larger number of the scares weren't credible.

Amanda Klinger, director of operations for the Educator's School Safety Network, said a few measures could help. Chief among them would be schools communicating with students about the severity of threats and parents reinforcing the message at home.

Am I sounding cynical? Let's read some thoughts from **Loyal Rue**, a professor of religion and philosophy at Luther College in Decorah, IA:

"**How** can one not be cynical when corruption in our government is so blatant and pervasive? It's not that we observe occasional specks of corruption in government—it is rather that our system of government is itself corrupt. We live now in what is officially an oligarchy. Citizens United was the tipping point and this insane new tax bill is the capstone.

"**To** be clear, this is not merely a rant about Trump and the clown car he emptied into Washington, D.C. This is older than Trump, deeper than Trump. I'm ranting here about a system of bribery and political extortion that renders this nation incapable of addressing the most serious problems facing our nation and the rest of the world."

"How can one not be cynical when all the earth's essential life-support systems— air, water, soil, biodiversity, climate – are in a critical state of decline, while our representatives in Washington cannot be bothered even to start serious conversations about the problems?"

"How can one not be cynical when no one in our government seems to get the point that you cannot get good legislation when politicians are beholding to uber-wealthy campaign donors?"

"Perhaps you think I should write to my congressional representatives? You think that's the answer? Give me a break. I'm from Iowa. Have you seen the caliber of political talent Iowans send to Washington?"

<u>Bus Driver Prayer</u>

May the roads be clear and the traffic not slow. May our drive not be hindered by rain, sleet or snow. May we reach safe and sound. All the places we go!

This cute little poem (above) was printed on a locally homemade plaque that was purchased in Branson, MO. It was a gift to me from one of my passengers during a great 4-day trip in 2011.

From our 2013 Colorado trip to visit. This is the Breckinridge area. Every turn will give you a breathtaking view.

Avolition is defined as lack of

initiative or motivation. In schizophrenia, when *avolition* is so severe as to prevent a person from doing ordinary things such as work, reading, or taking care of oneself, it is considered a "negative" symptom of the condition. With Bipolar II it just hangs around as a life-altering 'bad' habit!

Avolition can present itself in a number of ways:

1.) Being unable to start or complete paying bills.

2.) Staring at an assignment without getting to work on it.

3.) Just sitting for hours doing nothing.

7

Stigma

I spent 28 years working for a government agency that accepted bad behavior from its managers. I got an 'extra' four phony years added because I was a veteran with four years active duty in the U.S. Navy.

The **U.S. Postal Service** hiring pledge states that there will be no nepotism -- but, it is prevalent and running as rampant as ever in many cities. Crude and rude behavior is accepted in the workplace and anyone who complains gets removed, downgraded, or frozen in place for the remainder of their career. The multiple relationships and rapid marriages breaks that rule every time. *In-laws managing outlaws -- how clever.*

There was a time that I thought this bad behavior was just in the large post offices. I saw it in Detroit, Chicago, Orlando, Houston, Minneapolis. It was even showing up in small town Iowa, before I was forced into early retirement.

One headline reaction should be: *"DON'T LET STIGMA STOP YOU"*. What I mean is that the stigma, of actually talking about your strengths and weaknesses, can be a bridge to productive behavior.

I know that the stigma of telling

anyone about my bipolar thoughts and feelings cost me relationships, jobs and other opportunities. When I grew up in the 60's and 70's, the hint of mental illness was the death knell for your career. Story after story tells us about the abundance of prison inmates who are incarcerated, instead of in treatment, because they were and are too ashamed to admit to mental health struggles.

Suicide studies continue to report that the drastic, final solution is many times the result of someone too shy to ask for help.

We need to combat any misinformation about mental illness. Those afflicted do not deserve to be labeled as tainted or less worthy. Society is still too intolerant of people with psychiatric diagnosis. We need to continue to work to confront others with the facts of mental illness.

We need to work to overcome the mispercep

surrounding our interpersonal reactions to each other

This whole lazy process shows it's ugly head when trouble brews in our schools. The lack of discipline erodes the whole system. Kids learn little and they lose faith in adults when the loose status-quo is allowed to fester. And when kids lose faith in adults, they lose faith in life.

In Iowa, the news out of the State Senate is that they are working on a suicide prevention idea. School employees would be required to have training.

According to William Petroski, writer for the Des Moines Register, recently wrote that Iowa school employees would be required to take one hour of training in suicide awareness and prevention as a condition of renewing their state license or other certification under a bill approved amid emotional remarks in the Iowa Senate.

Senate File 2113 was approved 48-0, sending it to the House. Both Republican and Democratic lawmakers spoke about the suicides of young people, recalling tragic circumstances involving their families, friends and constituents in which they felt deep regret.

"This is a very important piece of legislation. As an educator, I have had to face that empty desk after a loss of a student. It is the most horrific thing that you can imagine," said Sen. Tod Bowman, a Democrat who teaches government at Maquoketa Community High School.

Bowman added that when people attend the funeral of a young person who has committed suicide, the question inevitably arises: "What could we have done to prevent this young person from taking their life?"

Sen. Brad Zaun, R-Urbandale, who mhas repeatedly pushed for suicide prevention efforts in response to teen suicides in the Johnston school district in 2012, said he recognizes that it often takes time for an issue to finally win approval in the Iowa Legislature. But he called the proposed legislation a good first step.

   "No one is patting themselves on the back. More needs to be done. We need to make mental health more of a priority in the state of Iowa," Zaun said.

   Sexual harassment is an everyday event. Everyone is afraid to speak up because that will put the label on you and your career is over. It is so prevalent that it is a 'given', when an attractive woman rises quickly through the ranks and her skills of handling the position that she is rewarded with. Just writing this statement makes me feel guilty of being complicit. But, it is so prevalent that the nickname 'Paragon of Mediocrity' fits the USPS.

   As I have said earlier, the term KMA (Kiss My Ass), first came to my attention as an early lesson in managing postal employees.

It was like this…"Don't try to talk sense into this guy, he is member of the KMA

Club!"

Most of the herd has been so used to
being treated poorly and dismissed during
any attempts of discussing a work subject,
that they have given up. They have given up
in giving a shit what the boss says. They
have given up on being any part of some
stupid team. They watch, over and over, how
the **"brown nosers"** and the **"suckups"** get
moved on up the ladder. Many management are
products of years of disregarding what is
good for the employee. Then when they get
promoted, they have no support from those
that they are put in charge of. This
frustration has turned into a national
phrase, now used in books and in
movies…GOING POSTAL. We all know what that
means.

USPS mental illness? Forget about that!
In a state wide district there may be one
person to counsel or advise. And when you
suggest that you need a mental health day,
you might as well forget about your name
coming up in any management discussions.

We now live in a climate of acceptance.
We put up with lack of discipline when the
kids come into school. We keep our hands off
and pass them along. We quietly accept rude
behavior at sporting events. We allow
parents to display bad judgement when their
kids are involved.

Up in Minnesota, teachers are trying
"restorative practices" in their approach to
discipline instead of suspending misbehaving
students.

Restorative practices aim to help students take responsibility for their actions while keeping them in the classroom. Teachers hold discussions daily in an effort to prevent bad behavior by getting students invested in doing the right thing. When students act out, the class is encouraged to talk about their feelings.

"It's a way that creates an opportunity for growth for individuals," said Nick Altringer, a teacher at Murray (MN) Middle School.. "The other way is more punitive, so it's always about harming the person and harming the person until they stop."

Six schools with the St. Paul Public Schools district each received $150,000 for additional staff, teacher training and informing parents of the new approach. The district extended funding and added three additional schools, with the hope of adding three more next year. The district has committed more than $4 million to the restorative practices projects over three years.

Area teachers began advocating the restorative practices two years ago as the district struggled with school discipline practices. Students of color were being disproportionally affected by suspensions. When the district tried to correct that practice, it found that it stopped enforcing consequences. Restorative practices are an effort to find a middle ground.

The school has used restorative methods for more than 30 cases, in 2017. District leaders said it's too early to tell how effective the new approach is.

Soon, on a Public TV station in your area, a real-life murder-mystery reenactment will appear with 1913 Floyd County Sheriff played by me.

90

8

Regrets

The lack of spine, in our elected officials, seem so apparent now. It's like night and day difference from when they were running for office. Now we learn who help pay for their election. Now we see their inaction on crucial legislation. Now we see where they continue to contradict the positions they took, earlier.

Here, in Iowa, the sell-out by our two very lazy and inactive Senators and Congressman. It is so obvious. The Des Moines Register has been drawn into writing editorials about these two.

Recently, The Register Editorial started with the headline: *"Give badge of shame to Young, Ernst"*.

The editorial was in response to the lack of action following the mass shooting in Florida. The editorial cited that the Florida students were right in targeting lawmakers who refuse to consider reasonable gun control measures.

> *Here are excerpts from that editorial:*

"Thoughts and prayers do not prevent schoolchildren from being slaughtered by gunman."

"Neither does calling a shooter "evil." Or ordering flags lowered to half-staff. Or other gestures offered by Iowa's GOP elected officials in the aftermath of a mass shooting as a Florida high school that left 17 people dead."

"Americans do not need more condolences, They need lawmakers, governors and President Donald Trump to finally support gun control measures experts say can save lives. These include barring weapon sales to violent criminals, banning semi-automatic weapons and limiting the amount of ammunition someone can purchase."

"Yet Republican Senator Joni Ernst says any federal action 'should focus on the root cause of the problem,' which she identifies as mental illness and substance abuse. 'We want to protect our Second Amendment right,' she felt compelled to note after the school shooting."

"The Second Amendment should not allow a troubled 19-year-old to legally purchase an AR-15. There is at least one Republican who understands this."

"Ohio Gov. John Kasich responded to the tragedy by encouraging 'common sense' gun regulations."

"But it appears the action will need to come from voters – who show up at the polls and kick out of office elected officials who reject common sense reforms. These politicians care more about campaign contributions from pro-gun groups than they do about the senseless and preventable deaths of thousands of Americans each year."

"The group of young people, from Florida, want to create a 'badge of shame' for politicians."

"Ernst should be among the first recipients of such a badge."

"The New York Times reported in October, 2017, that Ernst received more than \$3 million from the NRA, making her the seventh largest recipient of NRA funds currently in the U.S. Senate. Though she blames mental health and substance abuse for the mass shooting, she has supported a repeal of the same health reform law that provides the health insurance people need to access treatment."

No matter where I go, or where I strike up a conversation, the REGRET factor looms large in the trending conversations.

Inside the breakroom at the school bus barn the talk is always slanting towards the political. Some people think that they should have worked harder at getting out to vote, or getting others to get out and vote.

Then the oldest members of the breakroom stumble into their tired mantra that President Trump is doing all the things that they say THEY wanted to have done. Are you kidding? These somewhat normal people go from cheering the St. Louis Cardinals or the Chicago Cubs to total senility. When I ask for ONE concrete example of what Trump has done, they fall back on the old, "Well, he beat the liar Hillary!" Then they throw in, "You guys are still made that he beat Hillary!"

If you are over the age of 60, and you live in Iowa, you should be regretting the last election cycle.

The Des Moines Register has printed an Opinion, "State's GOP Leadership no friend to seniors."

The GOP's dedication to tax cuts and starving government has resulted in huge cuts to agencies designed to help vulnerable people. Unfortunately these agencies are headed by political appointees who do not consider seniors a priority either.

The Iowa Department on Aging now has 17 employees. Nine years ago (2009)it had 40 workers. Yet Director Linda Miller said she has not asked Gov. Kim Reynolds for additional funding, partly because the governor and her staff are already aware of the effect that the budget cuts are having.

The most recent proposed budget cuts to her agency are expected to result in 50,000 fewer meals delivered to the homes of these Iowans. Hundreds of older residents will see cuts in help obtaining everything from eyeglasses to utility assistance.

Down the hall is another state entity intended to assist seniors. The Iowa Long-Term Care Ombudsman's Office investigates complaints against nursing homes and assisted-living centers.

Except Iowans who call the office to report abuse or neglect are often routed to an automated messaging system telling them no one is available to take the call. Over the past 14 months, the office has shrunk from 17 employees to 12. Three vacant positions will not be filled.

Last summer budget cuts forced the

ombudsman's office to eliminate virtually all spending on travel.

Instead of visiting nursing homes in response to complaints about care, workers do investigations over the phone. This appears to directly violate state law, which requires the agency to "visit" long-term care facilities.

Do these public officials not understand government has a responsibility to do what it can to take care of people who cannot take care of themselves?

A state entity is supposed to respond when there are complaints about mistreatment in a nursing home. Our older neighbors who cannot leave their homes should be able to have a meal delivered. The reason long-term care ombudsmen is that everyone has long recognized seniors need someone on their side.

This shrinking of services for older Iowans comes as their ranks are mushrooming. Those 65 and older account for 16 percent of Iowa's population, the 14th-highest share in the nation as of 2015. The percentage is expected to reach 20 percent by 2050.

- I regret not listening in church. The main reason I went was because my mother said we had to. Also, the chance of sitting next to two of the five cheerleaders at our school was a HUGE incentive.

- I regret not finishing my Sunday School lessons. What I was I rebelling against?

- I regret not attending church on a regular basis.

- I regret not being more helpful around the house.

- I regret not asking for help.

- I regret not realizing my mental health dilemma.

- I regret not thinking many things through.

- I regret letting my mouth make me my "own worst enemy".

- I regret making excuses and thinking of the easy way to get around hard work.

- I regret being a very poor student in high school.

- I regret not having my hernia repaired until after it was too late to be anything special on the basketball floor, baseball diamond or the football field.

- I regret not talking seriously to my first girlfriend.

- I regret not being more thoughtful and thankful when that first serious girlfriend saved me from myself and lifted me out of a self-destructive path that I was on. I may have been fun and entertaining to be with, but I was hopelessly lost in my own feelings.

- I regret not getting into my good friends car, when he came to my house to drive us both to Mankato, MN, to join the Air Force on the 'buddy system". That was probably my first crucial mistake as I tumbled aimlessly for many years.

- I regret being a surprise father at 17. My early introduction to the thrill of alcohol hastened my start with destructive decisions.

- I regret running away from that responsibility and making fear of exposure and embarrassment more important than taking care of the baby girl.

- I regret acting out with speeding tickets and being jailed.

- I regret that overall shame of being a 3-time "jailbird" and hiding it from everyone.

- I regret moving to Minneapolis, chasing a new girlfriend, when I actually wanted to move to Hollywood. I still think I could have made something of myself had I ran away to California in the mid-60's.

- I regret my 50 year addiction to alcohol.

- I regret being an absentee father.

- I regret not being a better husband.

- I regret not taking better care of my mother.

- I regret not working harder at keeping our family together when my father died.

- I regret not being a better counselor during that hectic, rushed time that turned into the absolutely worst choice that my brother made when he quickly married his wife.

- I regret the many bad feelings I have had because my brother disappeared from my life, due to his wife's encouragement and his heavy drinking.

- I regret not working on my personal friendships.

- I regret driving drunk…so many, many times!

- I regret not pursuing legal action when I was rear ended in an accident, in Mankato, by a drunk driver. I was on my way to work at 5:00 AM. My Dad settled the claim for $1200. I still have back problems from that horrendous 'whiplash' accident.

- I regret signing off on a motorcycle accident for $850, because I was without guidance and the insurance company quickly waived some cash under my alcoholic nose!

- I regret not taking advantage of my position, following USN boot camp, after winning the American Spirit Honor Award. I drank myself from top recruit to troubled run-of-the-mill sailor.

- I regret not taking the US Navy opportunity to Yokusuka, Japan, where I would have been the NCO in charge of the US Navy broadcast studio for the Pacific Fleet.

- I regret not listening to financial advice from a good friend and a Navy Officer.

- I regret not investing in my future.

- I regret not taking the offered upper level communications postal jobs in Boston; Jacksonville, FL; Memphis, TN; Atlanta, GA; and the three at USPS Headquarters in Washington, DC.

- I regret moving to Iowa.

- I regret dropping out of the communications field and making the major mistake of accepting a position as Postmaster in Indianola. I have been out of my depth and lost since that fateful move in 1973.

- I regret transferring away from the Navy Reserves in Minneapolis.

- I regret transferring to the Army National Guard in Iowa.

- I regret not getting control on my casino addiction.

- I regret the many wasted days and night at casinos in Wisconsin and Minnesota.

- I regret the all-night casino runs.

- I regret not investing money earlier in life

- I regret not paying off my military taxes so I could have $420 more a month in retirement.

- I regret not staying in the Guard, as planned, for 28-30 years and climbing up to E-8 or E-9.

- I regret not filing my income taxes for past four years.

- I regret saying things that I did not mean.

Here is a timely and very appropriate Guest Column, from the Des Moines Register. The writer is Loyal Rue, a professor of religion and philosophy at Luther College, Decorah, IA.

"Dear Barack,

I miss you. I miss Michelle. I miss the feeling each morning that perhaps, after all, things will get better. I miss the sense of pride I once felt for my country. I miss your voice; the measured, thoughtful rhetoric I cannot recall ever hearing from a president. It gave me a sense of confidence and hope.

But the hope and confidence are now completely extinguished, leaving nothing but acidic cynicism. Now, when I recall your passionate remonstrations against cynicism, I feel my eyes rolling. Cynicism, I seem to recall you saying, is a cancer on the body politic. Somehow you managed to lure me out of my cynicism for several years, but now it's back, with all the lethargy and anger that comes with it.

How can one not be cynical when the corruption in our government is so blatant and pervasive? It's not that we observe occasional specks of corruption in government of government is itself corrupt. We live now in what is officially an oligarchy. Citizens United was the tipping point and this insane tax bill is the capstone.

To be clear, this is not merely a rant about Trump and the clown car he emptied into Washington, D.C., this year. This is older than Trump, deeper than Trump. I'm ranting here about a system of bribery and political extortion that renders this nation incapable of addressing the most serious problems facing our nation and the rest of the world.

How can one not be cynical when all the earth's essential life-support systems – air, water, soil, biodiversity, climate – are in critical state of decline, while our representatives in Washington cannot be bothered even to start serious conversations about the problems?

My life's situation appears to be summed up by *William Shakespeare* writing in **MacBeth** – **"Life's but a walking a shadow, a poor player that struts and frets his hour upon the stage. And then is heard no more; it is a tale told by an idiot, full of sound and fury, signifying nothing."**

9

Haunted

My own effort to fully embrace the KMA attitude has been honed throughout my life. So, it was not a far stretch for me to AGAIN give up on my life's pursuits when the idea of retirement came up.

Thanks to **Rodney Brooks** *(@Perfiguy)* writing for USA TODAY, he has laid out to a game plan on "How to prepare yourself to handle a tough transition."

Numerous surveys have shown that people think that they are going to retire later than it happens. The two big reasons: health issues and losing their job. According to the Employee Benefit Research Institute, 47% of American retirees retired before they planned, mostly because of health and disability.

I am personally haunted by the fact that I am too late to the party. I have missed the boat. That my erratic mental health will have passed away with no discernable change for my relatives that may be so afflicted.

One encouraging point of light is the

very recent spark in enthusiasm from a trio
of ladies in Des Moines. Des Moines Register
columnist Kathie Obradovich has already been
featured in an earlier discussion where she
was the moderator for a mental health forum
at Des Moines University. She has been
joined in this cause by two ladies with the
same last name. Huppert. More on that later.

Susan Huppert of Des Moines University

*Here is a 5-year-old picture from a photo shoot
in Waterloo, IA. The attractive young lady was
one representative of how ethnic people need to
care for their heart health. Me? What older,
overweight baby-boomers need to watch for!*

At age 54, a decade after his volunteer service as a nurse in the Civil War awakened him to the connection between the body and the spirit, **Walt Whitman** suffered a severe stroke that left him paralyzed. It took him two years to recover – convalescence aided greatly, he believed, ny his immersion in nature and its healing power. "How it all nourishes, lulls me," he exulted, "in a way most needed; open air, the rye-fields, the apple orchards."

The transcendent record of Whitman's communion with the natural world survives if ***Specimen Days*** (public library) – a sublime collection of prose fragments and diary entries, restoring the word "specimen" to its Latin origin in *specere*: "to look at." What emerges is a jubilant celebration of the <u>art of seeing</u>, so native to us yet so easily unlearned, eulogized with the singular electricity that vibrates in Whitman alone.

10

STUFF

As I have mentioned a number of areas
where our government has given up on
segments of the population, the most cruel
could be the wasting of food.

The numbers are staggering and hard to
comprehend. So I'll tone down the use of
numbers. Here, in the state of Iowa, the so-
called breadbasket of the world, we pitch
food into the trash left-and-right.

We have all seen it and ignored it.
Schools are one of the big culprits here. My
experience, locally, was working as an
Associate in Special Education at one of our
ten elementary schools. My size and
experience with kids got me extra duty as
lunchroom monitor. Easy stuff, like clean
off the tables and stop the kids from
throwing food at each other.

One position was standing next to a 30-
gallon container for the left-overs to go
into. Untouched Macaroni-and-cheese;
untouched apples; unopened cartons of milk;
five or six chicken nuggets; full slices of

bread. All into the garbage—unable to be recycled or shared. Health department rules? Habits? Fear of outbreak of ebola?

This was just in one of ten elementary schools in out 98% white, upper class community. Sometimes nicknamed "Swankeny".

A recent article in the Des Moines Register talked about how "Iowans toss food, recyclables at high rate".

Iowa's Department of Natural Resources sampled trash from 10 landfills and five transfer stations across Iowa for a study published in December 2017, looking to answer the question, "What are Iowans landfilling?"

According to Lauren Wade from IowaWatch.org, Tom Anderson, of the Iowa DNR's Land Quality Bureau and the study's project manager, has an answer to that question: **Money and jobs.**

Iowans dumped $60.3 million worth of recyclable materials into the state's landfills last year. Diverting those recyclables for the reuse could create more than 6,000 manufacturing jobs.

This is the fourth study of its kind published by the DNR since 1988, and showed that 20 percent of what Iowans landfilled in 2017 was compostable food waste. That was 6.7 percentage points higher than in a 2011 study. Seven percent of the food thrown into landfills still was packaged.

Another 10 percent of materials entering Iowa's landfills in 2017 – yard waste, for example – also could have been composted.

Following is an Editorial from the Des Moines Register.

The current Governor of Iowa, Kim Reynolds, appointed by outgoing Gov. Branstad on his way to be Trump's Ambassador to China, has continued to distinguish herself as someone who cares little for the poor or middle class.

A real KMA came recently as she blocked state regulators' plans and instead is hoping the Iowa Legislature would require safe storage of guns in child care centers. Because she refused to allow administrators to do their jobs, operators of child care centers and home daycares remain free to keep loaded weapons on the premises and not tell parents.

Keeping guns secure in a child care center does not infringe on anyone's Second Amendment rights. It is a matter of basic safety and common sense. That is likely why the vast majority of states have such a requirement. That is likely why no one from the public responded with a formal comment when DHS staff posted a standard "notice of intended action" about the rules last November.

But a lobbyist for the Iowa Firearms Coalition said he expressed concern to the governor's office, and Reynolds staff assured him the proposal was being put on hold. She publicly said she preferred that lawmakers decide the issue.

So how did leaving this up to the GOP-controlled Iowa Legislature work out?

A Democratic legislator introduced a bill, but it went nowhere. Republicans, who have worked to put more guns in the hands of more people to carry more places, were apparently not interested.

That is hardly a surprise. And thanks to the governor's allegiance to the gun lobby and her interference with basic rule-making, children and child care workers are less safe than they could be.

Probably my favorite scene over the past 20 years – any casino – makes no difference – I

> **get "high" as soon as I hear the machines working and see the lights flashing.**

My compulsion of choice are casinos. Anywhere and at any time. Cannot drive by. Love the look and the smell. More than 20 years! *Love the action and the noise.* Love the machines when they are paying out and hate them when they are not.

Locally, in central Iowa, we have Prairie Meadows. Some people may be surprised to learn that there are **19 casinos** in Iowa. Three are on Indian Reservations, with their own jurisdiction and policing.

Prairie Meadows is just outside of Des Moines, in the suburb of Altoona. A three-story gambling attraction disguised as a horse racing track.

Sometimes I have walked out with ATM slips showing me that I withdrew $300 and won NOTHING. Sick to my stomach. Afraid that my wife of 42 years will find out, and then I will have that terrible sinking feeling that a person gets when they are caught doing something wrong.

Just last week, I had $1,175 in my hand – BUT, did not get out before it was all gone. Like I guess a trance would feel like!

The Grandparent boom!

*A record 70 million Americans have
grandchildren.*

The Baby Boom has become the grandparent
boom: There are now more grandparents in the
U.S. than ever before – some 70 million,
according to the latest census. That's a 24
percent increase since 2001.

In fact, of all adults over 30, more than 1
in 3 were grandparents as of 2014.

Other than being great news for Hallmark –
maybe Grandparents Day will really catch on
– experts agree that the more grandparents
there are, the better for all involved.

"Grandparenting is healthy for us," says
Lillian Carson, author of the landmark book
The Essential Grandparent. "Being in touch
with the younger generation literally beefs
up the immune system."

The same boomers who famously doted on their
children are now lavishing attention on the
next generation—and with an average of 5 to
6 grandchildren per grandparent, that can
mean quite a financial investment. An AARP
study showed that 25 percent of grandparents
have spent more than $1,000 in the pst year
on their grandchildren. It is spent on gifts
as well as vacations: An entire travel
industry has now grown around
intergenerational travel.

It is all quintessential boomer
grandparenting, says **Grandparents.com**
columnist Barbara Graham.

"My mother loved my son. But there was
nothing like the level of obsession my

friends and I have for our grandchildren,"
Graham says.

**Special thanks to an online email
digest, titled *Brain Pickings*.
Researched and written by Maria Popova
at brainpickings.org.**

---

www.Pinterest.com/PMJIM

www.Facebook.com/James.Stordahl

Twitter.com/#!/PostmasterJim

http://askgrandpajim/blogspot.com/

IMDb.com/JamesStordahl (video clips)

Youtube.com/PostmasterJim (auditions)

www.nowcasting.com/JamesStordahl

www.dailykos.com/user/PostmasterJim

www.LinkedIn/In/grandpajim

When the Hollywood came to Iowa in 2008, I was the first local actor featured in a blog run by the Des Moines Register. The URL to the article:
http://blogs.desmoinesregister.com/dmr/index/php/2009/09/18/iowa-spotlight-take-one/

Social media that allows me to stay connected:

Twitter.com/#!/PostmasterJim

Youtube.com/PostmasterJim

http://www.IMDb.me/JamesStordahl

http://wwwJWSBoomervile.blogspot.com

http://www.helenwheels.net/cateye

http://www.dailykos.com/user/postmasterjim

http://www.LinkedIn.com/in/grandpajim

Facebook.com/James Stordahl

Pinterest.com/PostmasterJim

Google+/JamesStordahl

Jimthebusdriver.Weebly.com

Vine/PostmasterJim

Instagram/JamesStordahl

Skype/PostmasterJim

Thoughts gathered at the following locations:

Trinity Lutheran Church, Madelia, MN

Inside the home of Pastor Thor Skiei

Madelia, MN Grade School playground

Madelia, MN High School French class

Driving around Chris Jacobsen's house

<u>Junior year (1963), 11:45 AM, JFK assassination</u>

A pumpkin patch north of Madelia

Fedge Lake, outside Madelia, at Midnight

Mankato Outdoor Theater

An unknown location outside New Ulm, MN

Fox Lake Ballroom, Fairmont, MN

An unknown location in Mountain Lake, MN

George's Ballroom, New Ulm, MN

Kato Ballroom, Mankato, MN

The Johns family farm in New Ulm, MN

432 N. Jefferson Blvd., North Mankato, MN

Mankato (MN) State College

2101 – 3rd Ave. S., Minneapolis, MN

University of Minnesota

Rialto Theater, Mpls., MN

American Red Cross

Northwestern Hospital

Northwestern Hospital School of Nursing

2414 Elliot Ave. S., Minneapolis, MN

Blue and White Cab Company, Mpls.

Smith Ambulance

Olsen Ambulance

Twin City Limousine

James Ambulance

Walker, MN Chamber of Commerce

Leech Lake, Walker, MN

Hiawatha Beach Resort, Walker, MN

The Jolivette home, Hamilton, OH

US Army Boot Camp, Fort Ord, CA

US Navy Boot Camp, San Diego, CA

US Navy Reserves, OI Det 916

US Army Reserves, 409th INF, Walker, MN

Camp Ripley, MN

Fort McCoy, WI

Half dozen bars in LaCrosse, WI

US Army National Guard

The Julien home, 4628 - 30th Ave. S., Mpls.

Daytona Beach, FL

Drake University

USPS Bolger Management Academy, Bethesda, MD

Vincennes University, Indianapolis, IN

US Navy Postgraduate School, Monterrey, CA

Defense Information School, Fort Ben Harrison, Indianapolis, IN

Norfolk Naval Air Station

Commander-in-Chief, US Naval Reserve, New Orleans, LA

Atlantic Fleet Audiovisual Command, Norfolk, VA

USN Video news program "Telescope" studios

Norfolk Naval Base

The Pentagon

<u>US Postal Service Headquarters</u>

USPS Central Region HQ – Chicago

USPS Southern District HQ, Memphis, TN

National Postal Forum, Anaheim, CA

HMS Queen Mary, Anaheim, CA

Lakewood Church, Houston, TX

Crystal Cathedral, Anaheim, CA

Polynesian Cultural Center, Honolulu, HI

The countries of:

Mexico, Honduras, Panama,
Newfoundland, Yugoslavia, Portugal,
Italy, The Azores, and Canada.

A highlight in my life, which ended up in true bipolar fashion negative -- sitting in and fishing from the boat I WON on a $5 ticket! - this 16-ft Alumacraft Backtroller, with a 35-horse Evinrude outboard engine and trailer valued at $7,000 - we enjoyed this boat for 10 years - then I sold it for $2400 to temporarily catch up with gambling debts in Wisconsin.

Getting makeup touched up at local video taping of promotional piece for Iowa Public TV.

James Stordahl

Mike and Helen Stordahl
celebrating their wedding
anniversary.

One of my favorite photos of our early marriage, shot up at Walker, MN, after a successful fishing trip on Leech Lake.

The first weekend that all the girls met.

Nice shot of Jill and her soon-to-be new
husband, Darren Wolke.

Check out my two podcasts:

www.bipolardad.podbean.com

www.busbiz-libsyn.com

James Stordahl

9 781717 284167